Jack Joybubbles Spreads Joy!
Meet Jack Joybubbles

Written by
Diane Lopes

Illustrated by
Marta Maszkiewicz

Copyright © 2024 Diane Lopes, All rights reserved.
Illustrated by Marta Maszkiewicz

No part of this publication may be reproduced, stored in a retrieval system or transmitted in any form or by any means, electronic, mechanical, photocopying, recording or otherwise, without prior permission of Halo Publishing International.

For permission requests, write to the publisher, addressed "Attention: Permissions Coordinator," at the address below.

Halo Publishing International
7550 WIH-10 #800, PMB 2069,
San Antonio, TX 78229

First Edition, March 2024
ISBN: 978-1-63765-601-3
Library of Congress Control Number: 2024903719

Halo Publishing International is a self-publishing company that publishes adult fiction and non-fiction, children's literature, self-help, spiritual, and faith-based books. Do you have a book idea you would like us to consider publishing? Please visit www.halopublishing.com for more information.

In loving memory of Mackenzie B., who put the joy in Joybubbles and taught us how to have a Ding Dong Doodle Day. At the back of the book, I've included a couple of her Good Boy Cookie recipes, Jack's favorites.

And to my dad, Jack, who was an author himself and my inspiration to write this book.

Hi! I'm Jack. Jack **Joy**bubbles. **Joy**bubbles because I like to spread *joy*, and I really like bubbles.

I enjoy getting dressed up. My mom makes me the best bow ties and hats.

We like to share our Jack-tastic bow ties with our friends. They make everyone joyous. We call our friends Team Joybubbles.

We do lots of Jack-tivities every day!
I like to go on walks and take joyrides on our bikes.

My favorite Jack-tivity is eating cookies! Mom makes the BEST cookies. She calls them good-boy cookies.

We love to share our dandy, delicious cookies.
I enjoy eating them with my friends.

Spreading joy is so paw-some. Making bubbles is a great way to have fun and enjoy my friends.

Flying kites is an enjoyable way to spend the day.

Goodbye for now. Have a joyful
Ding Dong Doodle Day, everyone!

Banana-Carob Good Boy Cookies

1 Ripe Banana
1/2 cup Carob Powder
1-1/2 cup Whole Wheat Powder
3/4 cup Milk
1/4 cup Cornstarch

1. Preheat your oven to 350°F.
2. Mash the banana with a fork in a medium bowl.
3. Add the rest of the ingredients and mix well.
4. Roll dough on a lightly floured surface until it is 1/4-inch thick.
5. Cut dough using your choice of cookie cutters.
6. Place cookies on a nonstick baking sheet.
7. Pierce each cookie with a fork.
8. Bake for 10 to 15 minutes. If hard cookies are desired, continue to bake at 200°F until desired hardness is achieved.

Salmon-Pumpkin Good Boy Cookies

3 cups Wheat Flour
4 Eggs
1/2 cup Pumpkin Puree (substitutes: pureed sweet potato or squash)
1 cup Canned Salmon, drained
1 cup Coconut Oil, melted, but not hot

1. Preheat oven to 350°F.
2. Mix all ingredients together until an elastic dough is formed.
3. Add extra flour a little at a time if the dough is too sticky.
4. Turn dough out on a floured surface and roll to desired thickness.
5. Cut dough with your choice of cookie cutters.
6. Scrap dough pieces can be rolled into a rope and sliced into 1/2-inch segments. Press with your thumb.
7. Place cookies on a nonstick baking sheet and bake for 20 minutes.
8. Store in an air-tight container in the refrigerator.

www.ingramcontent.com/pod-product-compliance
Lightning Source LLC
Chambersburg PA
CBHW041439040426
42453CB00021B/2468